WANT MORE FROM YOUR JOURNAY TO SUCCESS USING THIS WORKBOOK. ACCESS THE ON DEMAND TRAINING VIDEO. DR. QUENCY WILL PROVIDES INSIGHTS TO ACHIEVING YOUR GOALS AND RALLYING THE SUPPORT IN YOUR LIFE.

SCAN ME

Sign up to create your username and login	→	Purchase On-Demand training Video	→	Download Design Life Hub App to from Apple & Google Stores

Introduction
EQUIPPED FOR SUCCESS

This vision planner is designed to support you not only achieving your goals, but maintaining. Traditionally, the approach to goal setting is knowing what you want and the steps you need to take for it to happen. The reality is taking the steps is not usually what pause or stop goal achievement. Is everything else.

"Equipped for Success" vision planner will help you look at creating a vision for your goal while also creating resources around the challenges you may face along the way. And not all challenges are bad, but they can be things that influence your success.

"Living a Life by design doesn't just happen. It comes by making the most of the highs and lows in life. Gleaming from it the resources that make you, YOU. And with the best you comes more than you could have imagined".
Dr. Q

Vision for PERSONAL GOALS

VISION

KNOWING YOUR VISION IS KEY TO GOING AFTER YOUR GOALS.
HERE YOU WILL EXPLORE HOW YOUR VISION IMPACTS OTHER AREAS OF LIFE.

WHAT ARE YOU LOOKING TO ACCOMPLISH?

	ADVANTAGES	DISADVANTAGES	OUTCOMES
WHO ELSE WILL BE IMPACTED			
OTHER LIFE AREAS IMPACTED			
PERSONAL CHANGES AS A RESULT			
WHAT IT REQUIRES TO MAKE CHANGE			

THE SOLUTION I CHOSE AND WHY

_____

_____

_____

VISION

ACTION BRAINSTORMING CAN HELP IDENTIFY THINGS THAT ARE HELPING OR HINDERING YOU FROM ACHIEVING YOUR GOALS.

MY GOAL:

STOP
DOING

DO
LESS OF

KEEP
DOING

DO
MORE OF

START
DOING

VISION TRACKER

GOAL:

PHASE:

january

1	2	3	4	5	6	7
8	9	10	11	12	13	14
15	16	17	18	19	20	21
22	23	24	25	26	27	28
29	30	31				

february

1	2	3	4	5	6	7
8	9	10	11	12	13	14
15	16	17	18	19	20	21
22	23	24	25	26	27	28
29						

march

1	2	3	4	5	6	7
8	9	10	11	12	13	14
15	16	17	18	19	20	21
22	23	24	25	26	27	28
29	30	31				

april

1	2	3	4	5	6	7
8	9	10	11	12	13	14
15	16	17	18	19	20	21
22	23	24	25	26	27	28
29	30					

NOTES:

VISION TRACKER

GOAL:

PHASE:

may

(1) (2) (3) (4) (5) (6) (7)
(8) (9) (10) (11) (12) (13) (14)
(15) (16) (17) (18) (19) (20) (21)
(22) (23) (24) (25) (26) (27) (28)
(29) (30) (31)

june

(1) (2) (3) (4) (5) (6) (7)
(8) (9) (10) (11) (12) (13) (14)
(15) (16) (17) (18) (19) (20) (21)
(22) (23) (24) (25) (26) (27) (28)
(29) (30)

july

(1) (2) (3) (4) (5) (6) (7)
(8) (9) (10) (11) (12) (13) (14)
(15) (16) (17) (18) (19) (20) (21)
(22) (23) (24) (25) (26) (27) (28)
(29) (30) (31)

august

(1) (2) (3) (4) (5) (6) (7)
(8) (9) (10) (11) (12) (13) (14)
(15) (16) (17) (18) (19) (20) (21)
(22) (23) (24) (25) (26) (27) (28)
(29) (30) (31)

NOTES:

VISION TRACKER

GOAL:

PHASE:

september

1	2	3	4	5	6	7
8	9	10	11	12	13	14
15	16	17	18	19	20	21
22	23	24	25	26	27	28
29	30					

october

1	2	3	4	5	6	7
8	9	10	11	12	13	14
15	16	17	18	19	20	21
22	23	24	25	26	27	28
29	30					

november

1	2	3	4	5	6	7
8	9	10	11	12	13	14
15	16	17	18	19	20	21
22	23	24	25	26	27	28
29	30					

december

1	2	3	4	5	6	7
8	9	10	11	12	13	14
15	16	17	18	19	20	21
22	23	24	25	26	27	28
29	30	31				

NOTES:

Look to make lasting changes. Break up your growth in phases. Master one phase before you move to the next level. The time in between phases can be long or short. The goal is mastery before going to the next level.

1
What is your first phase to change

....

....

2
What is your second phase to change

....

....

3
What is your third phase to change

....

....

4
What is your fourth phase to change

....

....

TASK LIST

GOAL

TASK LIST

- [ ] -
- [ ] -
- [ ] -
- [ ] -
- [ ] -
- [ ] -
- [ ] -
- [ ] -
- [ ] -
- [ ] -
- [ ] -
- [ ] -
- [ ] -
- [ ] -
- [ ] -
- [ ] -
- [ ] -

PRIORITIES

- [ ] -
- [ ] -
- [ ] -
- [ ] -
- [ ] -
- [ ] -
- [ ] -

NOTES

REMINDER

Head vs Heart

When considering the resources needed for growth and change, there is more to be considered than just the need to accomplish the goal. In this handout you will examine the role that your head and heart play when accomplishing a goal. You will also discover resources to support your growth.

HEAD

....

....

....

....

....

....

....

....

....

VS

HEART

....

....

....

....

....

....

....

....

....

Head & Heart Planner

Map the ways you will access your resources for reaching your goals as it relates to your head and heart. It's not enough to know what is going to keep you grounded. You must implement them regularly.

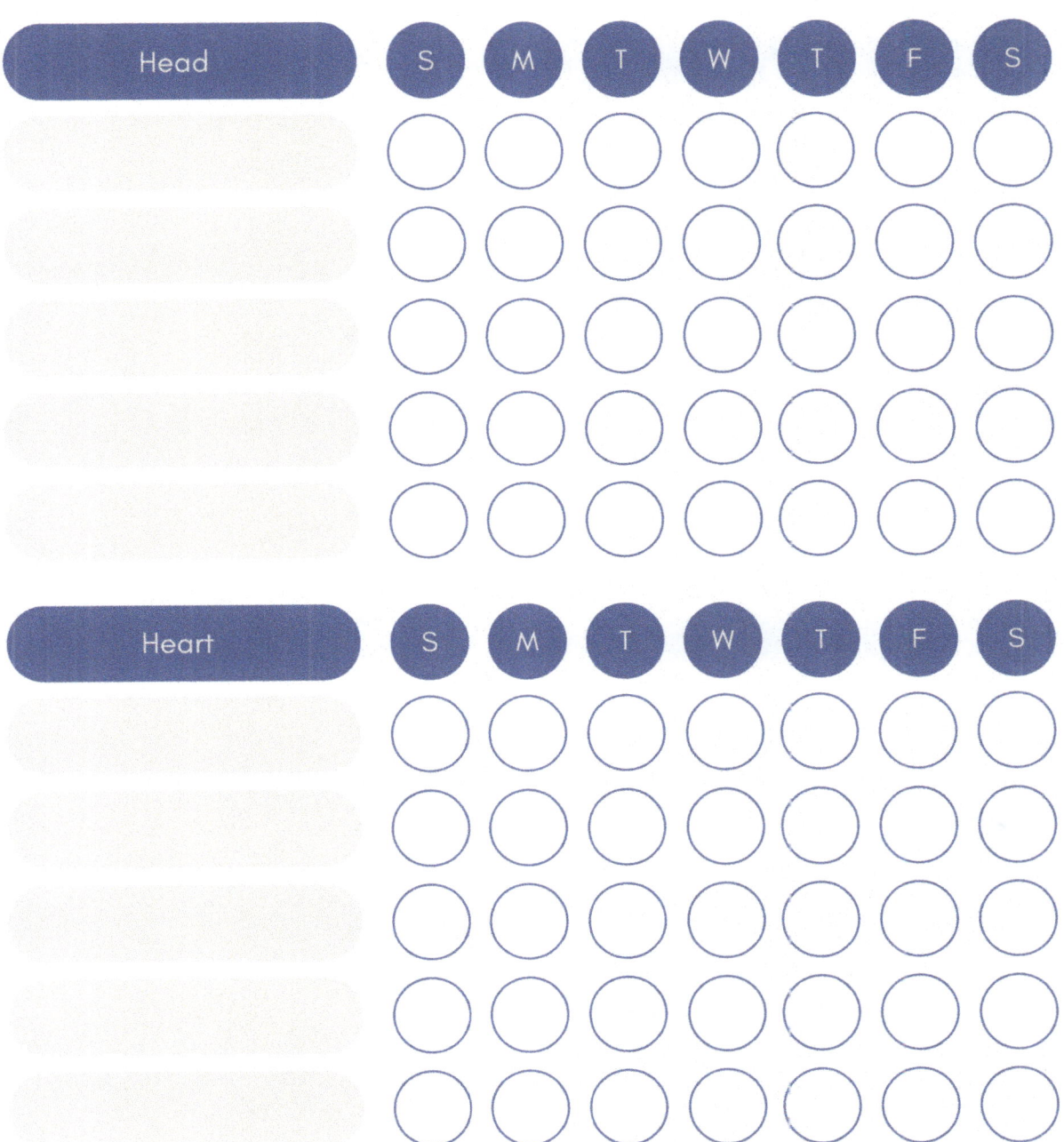

Head	S	M	T	W	T	F	S
	○	○	○	○	○	○	○
	○	○	○	○	○	○	○
	○	○	○	○	○	○	○
	○	○	○	○	○	○	○
	○	○	○	○	○	○	○

Heart	S	M	T	W	T	F	S
	○	○	○	○	○	○	○
	○	○	○	○	○	○	○
	○	○	○	○	○	○	○
	○	○	○	○	○	○	○
	○	○	○	○	○	○	○

COMMUNITY

REFLECT ON THE TYPE OF PEOPLE YOU NEED IN YOUR COMMUNITY FOR THE SEASON OF CHANGE YOU FIND YOURSELF IN. CONSIDER WHEN IT MAKES SENSE TO UTILIZE ONE COMMUNITY SUPPORTER OVER THE OTHER

CHEERLEADER

- [ ] CELEBRATES YOUR WINS
- [ ] SHOWS EXCITEMENT
- [ ] POSITIVE REFLECTIONS
- [ ] WANTS WHAT YOU WANT FOR YOURSELF
- [ ]

(WHO REPRESENTS THIS FOR YOU)

ACCOUNTABILITY

- [ ] STRETCHES YOU WHEN NEEDED
- [ ] KEEPS YOU ON TRACK
- [ ] VOICE OF TRUTH
- [ ] WON'T LET YOU GIVE UP
- [ ]

(WHO REPRESENTS THIS FOR YOU)

TEACHER

- [ ] PROVIDES INSIGHT
- [ ] HAS SUCCESS IN THE GOAL
- [ ] STYLE OF TEACHING MATCHES YOUR LEARNING STYLE
- [ ] PROVIDES RELEVANT RESOURCES
- [ ]

(WHO REPRESENTS THIS FOR YOU)

LISTENER

- [ ] FOCUSES ON WHAT YOU SHARE
- [ ] SAFE PLACE TO EXPRESS YOURSELF
- [ ] SUPPORTIVE
- [ ] CAN BE REFLECTIVE WITHOUT BEING DISCOURAGING
- [ ]

(WHO REPRESENTS THIS FOR YOU)

Note to Self

WRITE A NOTE TO YOUR SELF REFLECTING THE VALUE OF WHY YOU WANT TO ACHIEVE
THIS CHANGE IN YOUR LIFE

Note About Your Cheerleader

WRITE A NOTE ABOUT HOW YOU SEE YOUR CHEERLEADER AS A RESOURCE IN ACHIEVING YOUR GOAL

Note About Your Accountability

WRITE A NOTE ABOUT HOW YOU SEE YOUR ACCOUNTABILITY PERSON IS A RESOURCE
IN ACHIEVING YOUR GOAL

Note About Your Teacher

WRITE A NOTE ABOUT HOW YOU SEE YOUR TEACHER IS A RESOURCE IN ACHIEVING
YOUR GOAL

Note About Your Listener

WRITE A NOTE ABOUT HOW YOU SEE YOUR LISTENER IS A RESOURCE IN ACHIEVING YOUR GOAL

Vision for
FAMILY GOALS

VISION

KNOWING YOUR VISION IS KEY TO GOING AFTER YOUR GOALS.
HERE YOU WILL EXPLORE HOW YOUR VISION IMPACTS OTHER AREAS OF LIFE.

WHAT ARE YOU LOOKING TO ACCOMPLISH?

	ADVANTAGES	DISADVANTAGES	OUTCOMES
WHO ELSE WILL BE IMPACTED			
OTHER LIFE AREAS IMPACTED			
PERSONAL CHANGES AS A RESULT			
WHAT IT REQUIRES TO MAKE CHANGE			

THE SOLUTION I CHOSE AND WHY

_____

_____

_____

VISION

ACTION BRAINSTORMING CAN HELP IDENTIFY THINGS THAT ARE HELPING OR
HINDERING YOU FROM ACHIEVING YOUR GOALS.

MY GOAL:

STOP
DOING

DO
LESS OF

KEEP
DOING

DO
MORE OF

START
DOING

VISION TRACKER

GOAL:

PHASE:

january

(1) (2) (3) (4) (5) (6) (7)
(8) (9) (10) (11) (12) (13) (14)
(15) (16) (17) (18) (19) (20) (21)
(22) (23) (24) (25) (26) (27) (28)
(29) (30) (31)

february

(1) (2) (3) (4) (5) (6) (7)
(8) (9) (10) (11) (12) (13) (14)
(15) (16) (17) (18) (19) (20) (21)
(22) (23) (24) (25) (26) (27) (28)
(29)

march

(1) (2) (3) (4) (5) (6) (7)
(8) (9) (10) (11) (12) (13) (14)
(15) (16) (17) (18) (19) (20) (21)
(22) (23) (24) (25) (26) (27) (28)
(29) (30) (31)

april

(1) (2) (3) (4) (5) (6) (7)
(8) (9) (10) (11) (12) (13) (14)
(15) (16) (17) (18) (19) (20) (21)
(22) (23) (24) (25) (26) (27) (28)
(29) (30)

NOTES:

VISION TRACKER

GOAL:

PHASE:

may

1	2	3	4	5	6	7
8	9	10	11	12	13	14
15	16	17	18	19	20	21
22	23	24	25	26	27	28
29	30	31				

june

1	2	3	4	5	6	7
8	9	10	11	12	13	14
15	16	17	18	19	20	21
22	23	24	25	26	27	28
29	30					

july

1	2	3	4	5	6	7
8	9	10	11	12	13	14
15	16	17	18	19	20	21
22	23	24	25	26	27	28
29	30	31				

august

1	2	3	4	5	6	7
8	9	10	11	12	13	14
15	16	17	18	19	20	21
22	23	24	25	26	27	28
29	30	31				

NOTES:

VISION TRACKER

GOAL:

PHASE:

september

1	2	3	4	5	6	7
8	9	10	11	12	13	14
15	16	17	18	19	20	21
22	23	24	25	26	27	28
29	30					

october

1	2	3	4	5	6	7
8	9	10	11	12	13	14
15	16	17	18	19	20	21
22	23	24	25	26	27	28
29	30					

november

1	2	3	4	5	6	7
8	9	10	11	12	13	14
15	16	17	18	19	20	21
22	23	24	25	26	27	28
29	30					

december

1	2	3	4	5	6	7
8	9	10	11	12	13	14
15	16	17	18	19	20	21
22	23	24	25	26	27	28
29	30	31				

NOTES:

Habits

PHASES OF CHANGE

Look to make lasting changes. Break up your growth in phases. Master one phase before you move to the next level. The time in between phases can be long or short. The goal is mastery before going to the next level.

1

What is your first phase to change

....

....

2

What is your second phase to change

....

....

3

What is your third phase to change

....

....

4

What is your fourth phase to change

....

....

TASK LIST

GOAL

TASK LIST

- [ ] --
- [ ] --
- [ ] --
- [ ] --
- [ ] --
- [ ] --
- [ ] --
- [ ] --
- [ ] --
- [ ] --
- [ ] --
- [ ] --
- [ ] --
- [ ] --
- [ ] --
- [ ] --

PRIORITIES

- [ ] --
- [ ] --
- [ ] --
- [ ] --
- [ ] --
- [ ] --
- [ ] --

NOTES

REMINDER

Resources
Head vs Heart

When considering the resources needed for growth and change, there is more to be considered than just the need to accomplish the goal. In this handout you will examine the role that your head and heart play when accomplishing a goal. You will also discover resources to support your growth.

HEAD

....

....

....

....

....

....

....

....

....

VS

HEART

....

....

....

....

....

....

....

....

....

Head & Heart Planner

Map the ways you will access your resources for reaching your goals as it relates to your head and heart. It's not enough to know what is going to keep you grounded. You must implement them regularly.

COMMUNITY

REFLECT ON THE TYPE OF PEOPLE YOU NEED IN YOUR COMMUNITY FOR THE SEASON OF CHANGE YOU FIND YOURSELF IN. CONSIDER WHEN IT MAKES SENSE TO UTILIZE ONE COMMUNITY SUPPORTER OVER THE OTHER

CHEERLEADER

- [ ] CELEBRATES YOUR WINS
- [ ] SHOWS EXCITEMENT
- [ ] POSITIVE REFLECTIONS
- [ ] WANTS WHAT YOU WANT FOR YOURSELF
- [ ] ....
  (WHO REPRESENTS THIS FOR YOU)

ACCOUNTABILITY

- [ ] STRETCHES YOU WHEN NEEDED
- [ ] KEEPS YOU ON TRACK
- [ ] VOICE OF TRUTH
- [ ] WON'T LET YOU GIVE UP
- [ ] ....
  (WHO REPRESENTS THIS FOR YOU)

TEACHER

- [ ] PROVIDES INSIGHT
- [ ] HAS SUCCESS IN THE GOAL
- [ ] STYLE OF TEACHING MATCHES YOUR LEARNING STYLE
- [ ] PROVIDES RELEVANT RESOURCES
- [ ] ....
  (WHO REPRESENTS THIS FOR YOU)

LISTENER

- [ ] FOCUSES ON WHAT YOU SHARE
- [ ] SAFE PLACE TO EXPRESS YOURSELF
- [ ] SUPPORTIVE
- [ ] CAN BE REFLECTIVE WITHOUT BEING DISCOURAGING
- [ ] ....
  (WHO REPRESENTS THIS FOR YOU)

Note to Self

WRITE A NOTE TO YOUR SELF REFLECTING THE VALUE OF WHY YOU WANT TO ACHIEVE
THIS CHANGE IN YOUR LIFE

Note About Your Cheerleader

WRITE A NOTE ABOUT HOW YOU SEE YOUR CHEERLEADER AS A RESOURCE IN ACHIEVING YOUR GOAL

Note About Your Accountability

WRITE A NOTE ABOUT HOW YOU SEE YOUR ACCOUNTABILITY PERSON IS A RESOURCE
IN ACHIEVING YOUR GOAL

Note About Your Teacher

WRITE A NOTE ABOUT HOW YOU SEE YOUR TEACHER IS A RESOURCE IN ACHIEVING YOUR GOAL

Note About Your Listener

WRITE A NOTE ABOUT HOW YOU SEE YOUR LISTENER IS A RESOURCE IN ACHIEVING YOUR GOAL

Vision for
HEALTH GOALS

VISION

KNOWING YOUR VISION IS KEY TO GOING AFTER YOUR GOALS.
HERE YOU WILL EXPLORE HOW YOUR VISION IMPACTS OTHER AREAS OF LIFE.

WHAT ARE YOU LOOKING TO ACCOMPLISH?

	ADVANTAGES	DISADVANTAGES	OUTCOMES
WHO ELSE WILL BE IMPACTED			
OTHER LIFE AREAS IMPACTED			
PERSONAL CHANGES AS A RESULT			
WHAT IT REQUIRES TO MAKE CHANGE			

THE SOLUTION I CHOSE AND WHY

_____

_____

_____

VISION

ACTION BRAINSTORMING CAN HELP IDENTIFY THINGS THAT ARE HELPING OR HINDERING YOU FROM ACHIEVING YOUR GOALS.

MY GOAL:

STOP
DOING

DO
LESS OF

KEEP
DOING

DO
MORE OF

START
DOING

VISION TRACKER

GOAL:

PHASE:

january

(1) (2) (3) (4) (5) (6) (7)
(8) (9) (10) (11) (12) (13) (14)
(15) (16) (17) (18) (19) (20) (21)
(22) (23) (24) (25) (26) (27) (28)
(29) (30) (31)

february

(1) (2) (3) (4) (5) (6) (7)
(8) (9) (10) (11) (12) (13) (14)
(15) (16) (17) (18) (19) (20) (21)
(22) (23) (24) (25) (26) (27) (28)
(29)

march

(1) (2) (3) (4) (5) (6) (7)
(8) (9) (10) (11) (12) (13) (14)
(15) (16) (17) (18) (19) (20) (21)
(22) (23) (24) (25) (26) (27) (28)
(29) (30) (31)

april

(1) (2) (3) (4) (5) (6) (7)
(8) (9) (10) (11) (12) (13) (14)
(15) (16) (17) (18) (19) (20) (21)
(22) (23) (24) (25) (26) (27) (28)
(29) (30)

NOTES:

VISION TRACKER

GOAL:

PHASE:

may

(1) (2) (3) (4) (5) (6) (7)
(8) (9) (10) (11) (12) (13) (14)
(15) (16) (17) (18) (19) (20) (21)
(22) (23) (24) (25) (26) (27) (28)
(29) (30) (31)

june

(1) (2) (3) (4) (5) (6) (7)
(8) (9) (10) (11) (12) (13) (14)
(15) (16) (17) (18) (19) (20) (21)
(22) (23) (24) (25) (26) (27) (28)
(29) (30)

july

(1) (2) (3) (4) (5) (6) (7)
(8) (9) (10) (11) (12) (13) (14)
(15) (16) (17) (18) (19) (20) (21)
(22) (23) (24) (25) (26) (27) (28)
(29) (30) (31)

august

(1) (2) (3) (4) (5) (6) (7)
(8) (9) (10) (11) (12) (13) (14)
(15) (16) (17) (18) (19) (20) (21)
(22) (23) (24) (25) (26) (27) (28)
(29) (30) (31)

NOTES:

VISION TRACKER

GOAL:

PHASE:

september

(1) (2) (3) (4) (5) (6) (7)
(8) (9) (10) (11) (12) (13) (14)
(15) (16) (17) (18) (19) (20) (21)
(22) (23) (24) (25) (26) (27) (28)
(29) (30)

october

(1) (2) (3) (4) (5) (6) (7)
(8) (9) (10) (11) (12) (13) (14)
(15) (16) (17) (18) (19) (20) (21)
(22) (23) (24) (25) (26) (27) (28)
(29) (30)

november

(1) (2) (3) (4) (5) (6) (7)
(8) (9) (10) (11) (12) (13) (14)
(15) (16) (17) (18) (19) (20) (21)
(22) (23) (24) (25) (26) (27) (28)
(29) (30)

december

(1) (2) (3) (4) (5) (6) (7)
(8) (9) (10) (11) (12) (13) (14)
(15) (16) (17) (18) (19) (20) (21)
(22) (23) (24) (25) (26) (27) (28)
(29) (30) (31)

NOTES:

Habits

PHASES OF CHANGE

Look to make lasting changes. Break up your growth in phases. Master one phase before you move to the next level. The time in between phases can be long or short. The goal is mastery before going to the next level.

1 What is your first phase to change

....
....

2 What is your second phase to change

....
....

3 What is your third phase to change

....
....

4 What is your fourth phase to change

....
....

TASK LIST

GOAL

TASK LIST

- ☐ --------------------------------
- ☐ --------------------------------
- ☐ --------------------------------
- ☐ --------------------------------
- ☐ --------------------------------
- ☐ --------------------------------
- ☐ --------------------------------
- ☐ --------------------------------
- ☐ --------------------------------
- ☐ --------------------------------
- ☐ --------------------------------
- ☐ --------------------------------
- ☐ --------------------------------
- ☐ --------------------------------
- ☐ --------------------------------
- ☐ --------------------------------
- ☐ --------------------------------

PRIORITIES

- ☐ --------------------------------
- ☐ --------------------------------
- ☐ --------------------------------
- ☐ --------------------------------
- ☐ --------------------------------
- ☐ --------------------------------
- ☐ --------------------------------

NOTES

REMINDER

Resources
Head vs Heart

When considering the resources needed for growth and change, there is more to be considered than just the need to accomplish the goal. In this handout you will examine the role that your head and heart play when accomplishing a goal. You will also discover resources to support your growth.

HEAD

HEART

VS

Head & Heart Planner

Map the ways you will access your resources for reaching your goals as it relates to your head and heart. It's not enough to know what is going to keep you grounded. You must implement them regularly.

Head	S	M	T	W	T	F	S
	◯	◯	◯	◯	◯	◯	◯
	◯	◯	◯	◯	◯	◯	◯
	◯	◯	◯	◯	◯	◯	◯
	◯	◯	◯	◯	◯	◯	◯
	◯	◯	◯	◯	◯	◯	◯

Heart	S	M	T	W	T	F	S
	◯	◯	◯	◯	◯	◯	◯
	◯	◯	◯	◯	◯	◯	◯
	◯	◯	◯	◯	◯	◯	◯
	◯	◯	◯	◯	◯	◯	◯
	◯	◯	◯	◯	◯	◯	◯

COMMUNITY

REFLECT ON THE TYPE OF PEOPLE YOU NEED IN YOUR COMMUNITY FOR THE SEASON OF CHANGE YOU FIND YOURSELF IN. CONSIDER WHEN IT MAKES SENSE TO UTILIZE ONE COMMUNITY SUPPORTER OVER THE OTHER

CHEERLEADER

- [ ] CELEBRATES YOUR WINS
- [ ] SHOWS EXCITEMENT
- [ ] POSITIVE REFLECTIONS
- [ ] WANTS WHAT YOU WANT FOR YOURSELF
- [ ] (WHO REPRESENTS THIS FOR YOU)

ACCOUNTABILITY

- [ ] STRETCHES YOU WHEN NEEDED
- [ ] KEEPS YOU ON TRACK
- [ ] VOICE OF TRUTH
- [ ] WON'T LET YOU GIVE UP
- [ ] (WHO REPRESENTS THIS FOR YOU)

TEACHER

- [ ] PROVIDES INSIGHT
- [ ] HAS SUCCESS IN THE GOAL
- [ ] STYLE OF TEACHING MATCHES YOUR LEARNING STYLE
- [ ] PROVIDES RELEVANT RESOURCES
- [ ] (WHO REPRESENTS THIS FOR YOU)

LISTENER

- [ ] FOCUSES ON WHAT YOU SHARE
- [ ] SAFE PLACE TO EXPRESS YOURSELF
- [ ] SUPPORTIVE
- [ ] CAN BE REFLECTIVE WITHOUT BEING DISCOURAGING
- [ ] (WHO REPRESENTS THIS FOR YOU)

Note to Self

WRITE A NOTE TO YOUR SELF REFLECTING THE VALUE OF WHY YOU WANT TO ACHIEVE
THIS CHANGE IN YOUR LIFE

Note About Your Cheerleader

WRITE A NOTE ABOUT HOW YOU SEE YOUR CHEERLEADER AS A RESOURCE IN ACHIEVING YOUR GOAL

Note About Your Accountability

WRITE A NOTE ABOUT HOW YOU SEE YOUR ACCOUNTABILITY PERSON IS A RESOURCE IN ACHIEVING YOUR GOAL

Note About Your Teacher

WRITE A NOTE ABOUT HOW YOU SEE YOUR TEACHER IS A RESOURCE IN ACHIEVING YOUR GOAL

Note About Your Listener

WRITE A NOTE ABOUT HOW YOU SEE YOUR LISTENER IS A RESOURCE IN ACHIEVING
YOUR GOAL

Vision for
PROFESSIONAL GOALS

VISION

KNOWING YOUR VISION IS KEY TO GOING AFTER YOUR GOALS.
HERE YOU WILL EXPLORE HOW YOUR VISION IMPACTS OTHER AREAS OF LIFE.

WHAT ARE YOU LOOKING TO ACCOMPLISH?

	ADVANTAGES	DISADVANTAGES	OUTCOMES
WHO ELSE WILL BE IMPACTED			
OTHER LIFE AREAS IMPACTED			
PERSONAL CHANGES AS A RESULT			
WHAT IT REQUIRES TO MAKE CHANGE			

THE SOLUTION I CHOSE AND WHY

_____

_____

_____

VISION

ACTION BRAINSTORMING CAN HELP IDENTIFY THINGS THAT ARE HELPING OR HINDERING YOU FROM ACHIEVING YOUR GOALS.

MY GOAL:

STOP
DOING

DO
LESS OF

KEEP
DOING

DO
MORE OF

START
DOING

VISION TRACKER

GOAL:

PHASE:

january

(1) (2) (3) (4) (5) (6) (7)
(8) (9) (10) (11) (12) (13) (14)
(15) (16) (17) (18) (19) (20) (21)
(22) (23) (24) (25) (26) (27) (28)
(29) (30) (31)

february

(1) (2) (3) (4) (5) (6) (7)
(8) (9) (10) (11) (12) (13) (14)
(15) (16) (17) (18) (19) (20) (21)
(22) (23) (24) (25) (26) (27) (28)
(29)

march

(1) (2) (3) (4) (5) (6) (7)
(8) (9) (10) (11) (12) (13) (14)
(15) (16) (17) (18) (19) (20) (21)
(22) (23) (24) (25) (26) (27) (28)
(29) (30) (31)

april

(1) (2) (3) (4) (5) (6) (7)
(8) (9) (10) (11) (12) (13) (14)
(15) (16) (17) (18) (19) (20) (21)
(22) (23) (24) (25) (26) (27) (28)
(29) (30)

NOTES:

VISION TRACKER

GOAL:

PHASE:

may

1	2	3	4	5	6	7
8	9	10	11	12	13	14
15	16	17	18	19	20	21
22	23	24	25	26	27	28
29	30	31				

june

1	2	3	4	5	6	7
8	9	10	11	12	13	14
15	16	17	18	19	20	21
22	23	24	25	26	27	28
29	30					

july

1	2	3	4	5	6	7
8	9	10	11	12	13	14
15	16	17	18	19	20	21
22	23	24	25	26	27	28
29	30	31				

august

1	2	3	4	5	6	7
8	9	10	11	12	13	14
15	16	17	18	19	20	21
22	23	24	25	26	27	28
29	30	31				

NOTES:

VISION TRACKER

GOAL:

PHASE:

september

① ② ③ ④ ⑤ ⑥ ⑦
⑧ ⑨ ⑩ ⑪ ⑫ ⑬ ⑭
⑮ ⑯ ⑰ ⑱ ⑲ ⑳ ㉑
㉒ ㉓ ㉔ ㉕ ㉖ ㉗ ㉘
㉙ ㉚

october

① ② ③ ④ ⑤ ⑥ ⑦
⑧ ⑨ ⑩ ⑪ ⑫ ⑬ ⑭
⑮ ⑯ ⑰ ⑱ ⑲ ⑳ ㉑
㉒ ㉓ ㉔ ㉕ ㉖ ㉗ ㉘
㉙ ㉚

november

① ② ③ ④ ⑤ ⑥ ⑦
⑧ ⑨ ⑩ ⑪ ⑫ ⑬ ⑭
⑮ ⑯ ⑰ ⑱ ⑲ ⑳ ㉑
㉒ ㉓ ㉔ ㉕ ㉖ ㉗ ㉘
㉙ ㉚

december

① ② ③ ④ ⑤ ⑥ ⑦
⑧ ⑨ ⑩ ⑪ ⑫ ⑬ ⑭
⑮ ⑯ ⑰ ⑱ ⑲ ⑳ ㉑
㉒ ㉓ ㉔ ㉕ ㉖ ㉗ ㉘
㉙ ㉚ ㉛

NOTES:

Habits
PHASES OF CHANGE

Look to make lasting changes. Break up your growth in phases. Master one phase before you move to the next level. The time in between phases can be long or short. The goal is mastery before going to the next level.

1
What is your first phase to change

....

....

2
What is your second phase to change

....

....

3
What is your third phase to change

....

....

4
What is your fourth phase to change

....

....

TASK LIST

GOAL

TASK LIST

- [ ] --------------------------------
- [ ] --------------------------------
- [ ] --------------------------------
- [ ] --------------------------------
- [ ] --------------------------------
- [ ] --------------------------------
- [ ] --------------------------------
- [ ] --------------------------------
- [ ] --------------------------------
- [ ] --------------------------------
- [ ] --------------------------------
- [ ] --------------------------------
- [ ] --------------------------------
- [ ] --------------------------------
- [ ] --------------------------------
- [ ] --------------------------------
- [ ] --------------------------------
- [ ] --------------------------------

PRIORITIES

- [ ] --------------------------------
- [ ] --------------------------------
- [ ] --------------------------------
- [ ] --------------------------------
- [ ] --------------------------------
- [ ] --------------------------------
- [ ] --------------------------------

NOTES

REMINDER

Resources

Head vs Heart

When considering the resources needed for growth and change, there is more to be considered than just the need to accomplish the goal. In this handout you will examine the role that your head and heart play when accomplishing a goal. You will also discover resources to support your growth.

HEAD

HEART

VS

Head & Heart Planner

Map the ways you will access your resources for reaching your goals as it relates to your head and heart. It's not enough to know what is going to keep you grounded. You must implement them regularly.

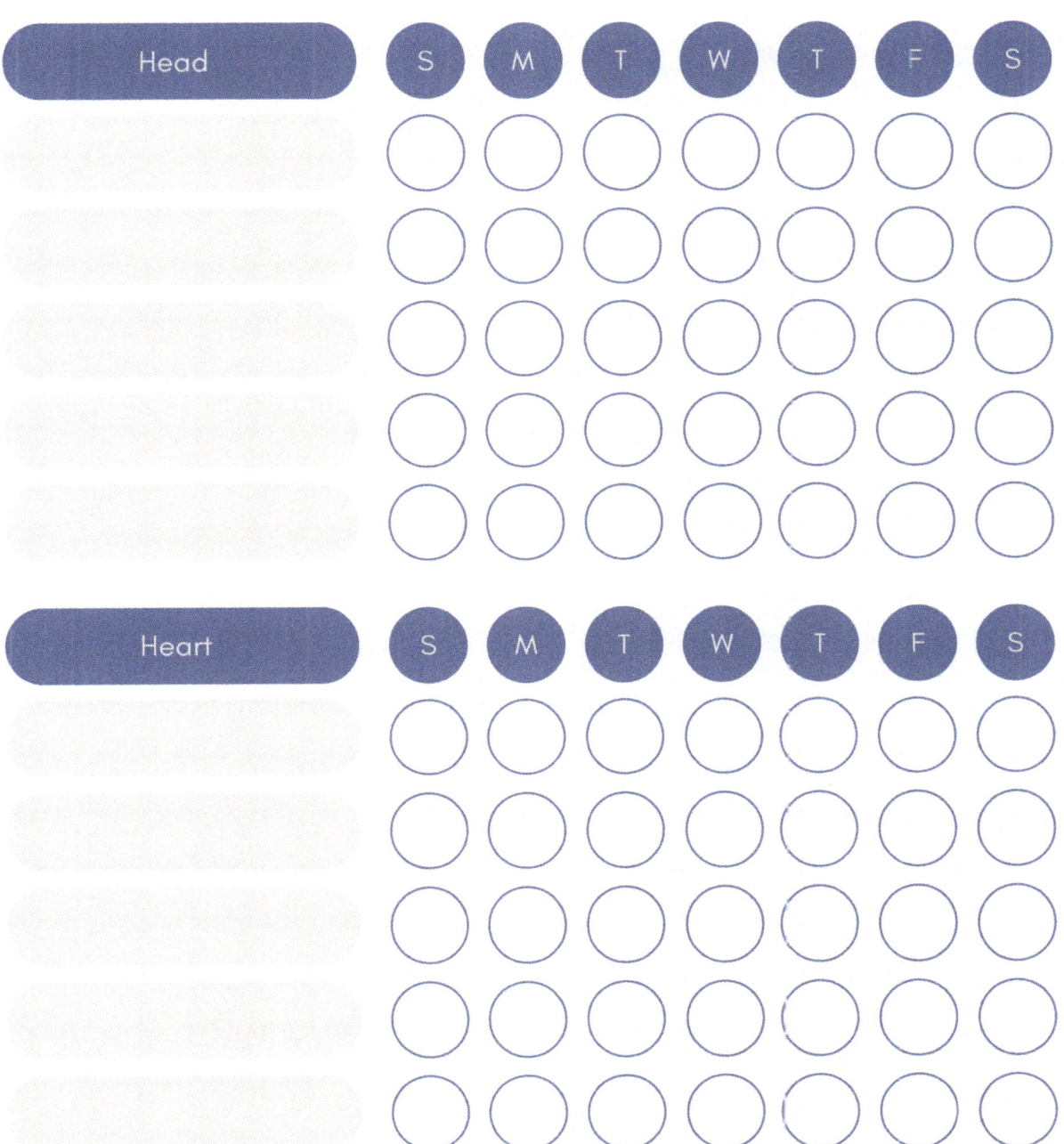

Head	S	M	T	W	T	F	S
	○	○	○	○	○	○	○
	○	○	○	○	○	○	○
	○	○	○	○	○	○	○
	○	○	○	○	○	○	○
	○	○	○	○	○	○	○

Heart	S	M	T	W	T	F	S
	○	○	○	○	○	○	○
	○	○	○	○	○	○	○
	○	○	○	○	○	○	○
	○	○	○	○	○	○	○
	○	○	○	○	○	○	○

COMMUNITY

REFLECT ON THE TYPE OF PEOPLE YOU NEED IN YOUR COMMUNITY FOR THE SEASON OF CHANGE YOU FIND YOURSELF IN. CONSIDER WHEN IT MAKES SENSE TO UTILIZE ONE COMMUNITY SUPPORTER OVER THE OTHER

CHEERLEADER

- [ ] CELEBRATES YOUR WINS
- [ ] SHOWS EXCITEMENT
- [ ] POSITIVE REFLECTIONS
- [ ] WANTS WHAT YOU WANT FOR YOURSELF
- [ ] ....
(WHO REPRESENTS THIS FOR YOU)

ACCOUNTABILITY

- [ ] STRETCHES YOU WHEN NEEDED
- [ ] KEEPS YOU ON TRACK
- [ ] VOICE OF TRUTH
- [ ] WON'T LET YOU GIVE UP
- [ ] ....
(WHO REPRESENTS THIS FOR YOU)

TEACHER

- [ ] PROVIDES INSIGHT
- [ ] HAS SUCCESS IN THE GOAL
- [ ] STYLE OF TEACHING MATCHES YOUR LEARNING STYLE
- [ ] PROVIDES RELEVANT RESOURCES
- [ ] ....
(WHO REPRESENTS THIS FOR YOU)

LISTENER

- [ ] FOCUSES ON WHAT YOU SHARE
- [ ] SAFE PLACE TO EXPRESS YOURSELF
- [ ] SUPPORTIVE
- [ ] CAN BE REFLECTIVE WITHOUT BEING DISCOURAGING
- [ ] ....
(WHO REPRESENTS THIS FOR YOU)

Note to Self

WRITE A NOTE TO YOUR SELF REFLECTING THE VALUE OF WHY YOU WANT TO ACHIEVE
THIS CHANGE IN YOUR LIFE

....

....

....

....

....

....

....

....

....

....

....

....

....

....

Note About Your Cheerleader

WRITE A NOTE ABOUT HOW YOU SEE YOUR CHEERLEADER AS A RESOURCE IN
ACHIEVING YOUR GOAL

Note About Your Accountability

WRITE A NOTE ABOUT HOW YOU SEE YOUR ACCOUNTABILITY PERSON IS A RESOURCE
IN ACHIEVING YOUR GOAL

Note About Your Teacher

WRITE A NOTE ABOUT HOW YOU SEE YOUR TEACHER IS A RESOURCE IN ACHIEVING YOUR GOAL

Note About Your Listener

WRITE A NOTE ABOUT HOW YOU SEE YOUR LISTENER IS A RESOURCE IN ACHIEVING YOUR GOAL

Vision for
OTHER GOALS

VISION

KNOWING YOUR VISION IS KEY TO GOING AFTER YOUR GOALS.
HERE YOU WILL EXPLORE HOW YOUR VISION IMPACTS OTHER AREAS OF LIFE.

WHAT ARE YOU LOOKING TO ACCOMPLISH?

	ADVANTAGES	DISADVANTAGES	OUTCOMES
WHO ELSE WILL BE IMPACTED			
OTHER LIFE AREAS IMPACTED			
PERSONAL CHANGES AS A RESULT			
WHAT IT REQUIRES TO MAKE CHANGE			

THE SOLUTION I CHOSE AND WHY

_____

_____

_____

VISION

ACTION BRAINSTORMING CAN HELP IDENTIFY THINGS THAT ARE HELPING OR
HINDERING YOU FROM ACHIEVING YOUR GOALS.

MY GOAL:

STOP
DOING

DO
LESS OF

KEEP
DOING

DO
MORE OF

START
DOING

VISION TRACKER

GOAL:

PHASE:

january

(1) (2) (3) (4) (5) (6) (7)
(8) (9) (10) (11) (12) (13) (14)
(15) (16) (17) (18) (19) (20) (21)
(22) (23) (24) (25) (26) (27) (28)
(29) (30) (31)

february

(1) (2) (3) (4) (5) (6) (7)
(8) (9) (10) (11) (12) (13) (14)
(15) (16) (17) (18) (19) (20) (21)
(22) (23) (24) (25) (26) (27) (28)
(29)

march

(1) (2) (3) (4) (5) (6) (7)
(8) (9) (10) (11) (12) (13) (14)
(15) (16) (17) (18) (19) (20) (21)
(22) (23) (24) (25) (26) (27) (28)
(29) (30) (31)

april

(1) (2) (3) (4) (5) (6) (7)
(8) (9) (10) (11) (12) (13) (14)
(15) (16) (17) (18) (19) (20) (21)
(22) (23) (24) (25) (26) (27) (28)
(29) (30)

NOTES:

VISION TRACKER

GOAL:

PHASE:

may

1	2	3	4	5	6	7
8	9	10	11	12	13	14
15	16	17	18	19	20	21
22	23	24	25	26	27	28
29	30	31				

june

1	2	3	4	5	6	7
8	9	10	11	12	13	14
15	16	17	18	19	20	21
22	23	24	25	26	27	28
29	30					

july

1	2	3	4	5	6	7
8	9	10	11	12	13	14
15	16	17	18	19	20	21
22	23	24	25	26	27	28
29	30	31				

august

1	2	3	4	5	6	7
8	9	10	11	12	13	14
15	16	17	18	19	20	21
22	23	24	25	26	27	28
29	30	31				

NOTES:

VISION TRACKER

GOAL:

PHASE:

september

1	2	3	4	5	6	7
8	9	10	11	12	13	14
15	16	17	18	19	20	21
22	23	24	25	26	27	28
29	30					

october

1	2	3	4	5	6	7
8	9	10	11	12	13	14
15	16	17	18	19	20	21
22	23	24	25	26	27	28
29	30					

november

1	2	3	4	5	6	7
8	9	10	11	12	13	14
15	16	17	18	19	20	21
22	23	24	25	26	27	28
29	30					

december

1	2	3	4	5	6	7
8	9	10	11	12	13	14
15	16	17	18	19	20	21
22	23	24	25	26	27	28
29	30	31				

NOTES:

Habits

PHASES OF CHANGE

Look to make lasting changes. Break up your growth in phases. Master one phase before you move to the next level. The time in between phases can be long or short. The goal is mastery before going to the next level.

1 What is your first phase to change

....

....

2 What is your second phase to change

....

....

3 What is your third phase to change

....

....

4 What is your fourth phase to change

....

....

TASK LIST

GOAL

TASK LIST

- [ ] --------------------------------
- [ ] --------------------------------
- [ ] --------------------------------
- [ ] --------------------------------
- [ ] --------------------------------
- [ ] --------------------------------
- [ ] --------------------------------
- [ ] --------------------------------
- [ ] --------------------------------
- [ ] --------------------------------
- [ ] --------------------------------
- [ ] --------------------------------
- [ ] --------------------------------
- [ ] --------------------------------
- [ ] --------------------------------
- [ ] --------------------------------
- [ ] --------------------------------

PRIORITIES

- [ ] --------------------------------
- [ ] --------------------------------
- [ ] --------------------------------
- [ ] --------------------------------
- [ ] --------------------------------
- [ ] --------------------------------
- [ ] --------------------------------

NOTES

REMINDER

Head vs Heart

When considering the resources needed for growth and change, there is more to be considered than just the need to accomplish the goal. In this handout you will examine the role that your head and heart play when accomplishing a goal. You will also discover resources to support your growth.

HEAD

....

....

....

....

....

....

....

....

....

VS

HEART

....

....

....

....

....

....

....

....

....

Head & Heart Planner

Map the ways you will access your resources for reaching your goals as it relates to your head and heart. It's not enough to know what is going to keep you grounded. You must implement them regularly.

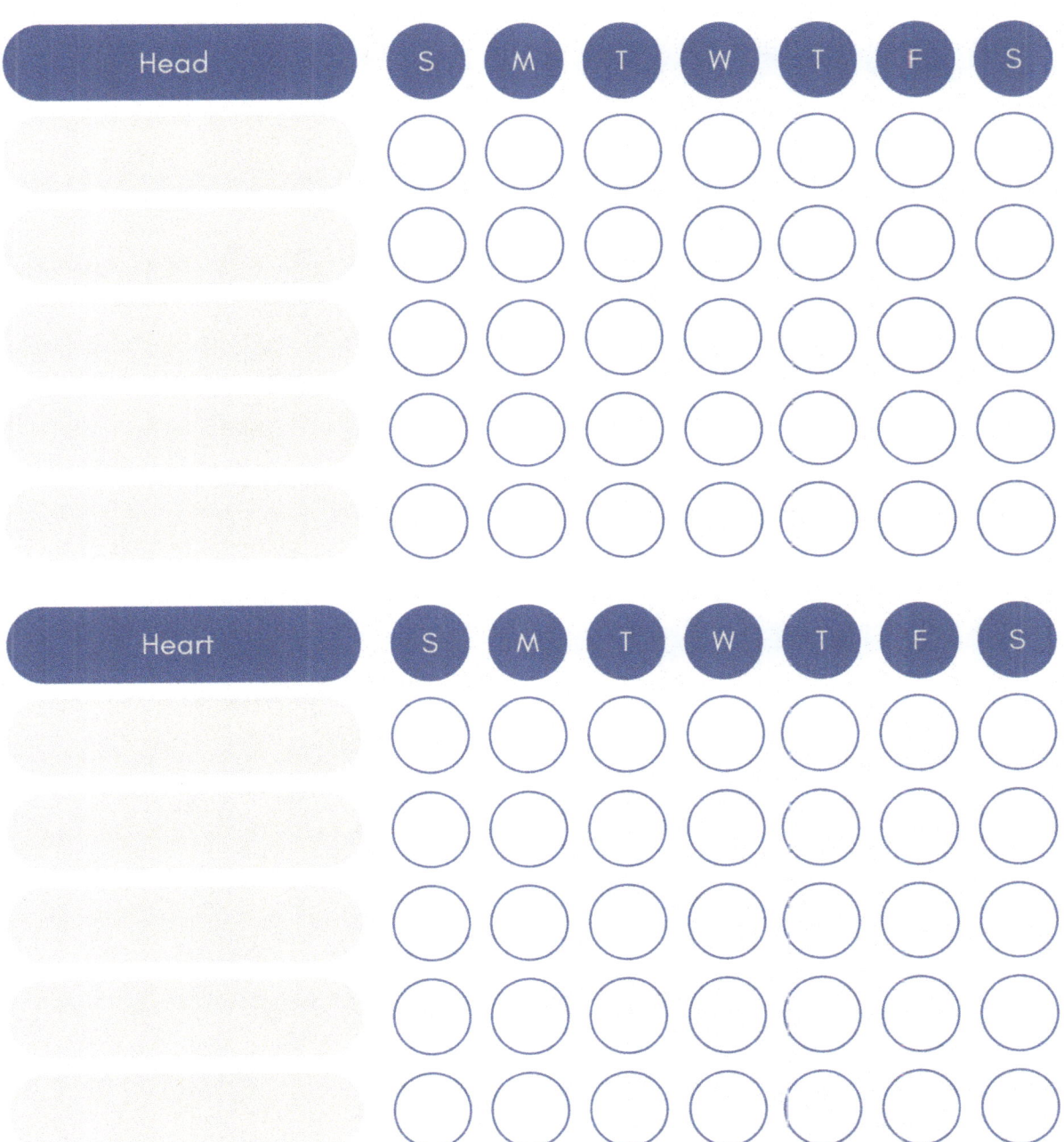

Head	S	M	T	W	T	F	S
	○	○	○	○	○	○	○
	○	○	○	○	○	○	○
	○	○	○	○	○	○	○
	○	○	○	○	○	○	○
	○	○	○	○	○	○	○

Heart	S	M	T	W	T	F	S
	○	○	○	○	○	○	○
	○	○	○	○	○	○	○
	○	○	○	○	○	○	○
	○	○	○	○	○	○	○
	○	○	○	○	○	○	○

COMMUNITY

REFLECT ON THE TYPE OF PEOPLE YOU NEED IN YOUR COMMUNITY FOR THE SEASON OF CHANGE YOU FIND YOURSELF IN. CONSIDER WHEN IT MAKES SENSE TO UTILIZE ONE COMMUNITY SUPPORTER OVER THE OTHER

CHEERLEADER

- [ ] CELEBRATES YOUR WINS
- [ ] SHOWS EXCITEMENT
- [ ] POSITIVE REFLECTIONS
- [ ] WANTS WHAT YOU WANT FOR YOURSELF
- [ ] ....
  (WHO REPRESENTS THIS FOR YOU)

ACCOUNTABILITY

- [ ] STRETCHES YOU WHEN NEEDED
- [ ] KEEPS YOU ON TRACK
- [ ] VOICE OF TRUTH
- [ ] WON'T LET YOU GIVE UP
- [ ] ....
  (WHO REPRESENTS THIS FOR YOU)

TEACHER

- [ ] PROVIDES INSIGHT
- [ ] HAS SUCCESS IN THE GOAL
- [ ] STYLE OF TEACHING MATCHES YOUR LEARNING STYLE
- [ ] PROVIDES RELEVANT RESOURCES
- [ ] ....
  (WHO REPRESENTS THIS FOR YOU)

LISTENER

- [ ] FOCUSES ON WHAT YOU SHARE
- [ ] SAFE PLACE TO EXPRESS YOURSELF
- [ ] SUPPORTIVE
- [ ] CAN BE REFLECTIVE WITHOUT BEING DISCOURAGING
- [ ] ....
  (WHO REPRESENTS THIS FOR YOU)

Note to Self

WRITE A NOTE TO YOUR SELF REFLECTING THE VALUE OF WHY YOU WANT TO ACHIEVE
THIS CHANGE IN YOUR LIFE

Note About Your Cheerleader

WRITE A NOTE ABOUT HOW YOU SEE YOUR CHEERLEADER AS A RESOURCE IN
ACHIEVING YOUR GOAL

Note About Your Accountability

WRITE A NOTE ABOUT HOW YOU SEE YOUR ACCOUNTABILITY PERSON IS A RESOURCE
IN ACHIEVING YOUR GOAL

....

....

....

....

....

....

....

....

....

....

....

....

....

....

Note About Your Teacher

WRITE A NOTE ABOUT HOW YOU SEE YOUR TEACHER IS A RESOURCE IN ACHIEVING
YOUR GOAL

Note About Your Listener

WRITE A NOTE ABOUT HOW YOU SEE YOUR LISTENER IS A RESOURCE IN ACHIEVING YOUR GOAL

THANK YOU

Thank you for your purchase! If you have enjoyed this purchase please consider dropping us a review. It takes 5 seconds and helps a small business like ours.

Design Life Hub Resources

LEARN MORE

About Design Life Hub

Program Plan Information

Stay Connected

Apple Store

Google Play Store

Facebook

Instagram